April 23, 2015

Objective

Our objective was to determine whether Space and Naval Warfare Systems Command (SPAWAR) contracting officials provided a fair opportunity to compete, supported price reasonableness determinations, and performed surveillance for task orders issued under multiple-award contracts for services and in accordance with Federal and DoD procedures. We reviewed a nonstatistical sample of 20 task orders from the multiple-award contracts awarded by SPAWAR Systems Center Pacific valued at $39.7 million.

Finding

SPAWAR officials generally provided a fair opportunity to compete, supported price reasonableness determinations, and performed surveillance for the global installation nonstatistically selected contracts and task orders. Officials also generally awarded and managed the task orders in accordance with regulations; however, some improvements are needed. Specifically contracting officials did not:

- properly designate contracting officer's representatives (COR) because they did not prepare designation letters as required;

- verify contractor employees had the proper certifications because officials relied on contractor statements and subsequent COR spot checks; or

Finding (cont'd)

- close out task orders in a timely manner because officials did not always receive contractor's completion reports, internal performance reviews, and funding reports.

As a result, SPAWAR officials increased cost and performance risk on the contract and may delay the return of funds that could be put to better use by not closing out the task orders in a timely manner.

Recommendations

We recommend that the SPAWAR Global Installation Contracts Contracting Officer verify that proposed CORs have the required training and properly designate all CORs before they perform oversight of a task order; revise the Quality Assurance Surveillance Plan to contain procedures for CORs to verify all contractor employees have required certifications. Further, we recommend that the contracting officer review and update the task order closeout process.

Management Comments and Our Response

The Deputy Assistant Secretary of the Navy (Acquisition & Procurement), responding for Space and Naval Warfare Systems Command, Global Installation Contracts, Contracting Officer, addressed all specifics of the recommendations, and no further comments are required. Please see the Recommendations Table on the back of this page.

Recommendations Table

Management	Recommendations Requiring Comment	No Additional Comments Required
Space and Naval Warfare Command, Global Installation Contracts, Contracting Officer		1.a, 1.b, 1.c, 1.d

INSPECTOR GENERAL
DEPARTMENT OF DEFENSE
4800 MARK CENTER DRIVE
ALEXANDRIA, VIRGINIA 22350-1500

April 23, 2015

MEMORANDUM FOR UNDER SECRETARY OF DEFENSE FOR ACQUISITION,
TECHNOLOGY, AND LOGISTICS
NAVAL INSPECTOR GENERAL

SUBJECT: Administration of Space and Naval Warfare Systems Command Global Installation
Multiple-Award Contracts Can Be Improved (Report No. DODIG-2015-109)

We are providing this report for your information and use. Space and Naval Warfare
Systems Command officials generally provided a fair opportunity to compete, supported
price reasonableness, and performed surveillance for the global installation contracts and
task orders in our sample, valued at $39.7 million. However, officials did not properly
designate all contracting officer's representatives, verify all contractor employees had the
required certifications, or close out task orders in a timely manner. We conducted this audit
in accordance with generally accepted government auditing standards.

We considered management comments on a draft of this report when preparing the
final report. Comments from the Deputy Assistant Secretary of the Navy (Acquisition &
Procurement), responding for Space and Naval Warfare Systems Command, Global Installation
Contracts, Contracting Officer, conformed to the requirements of DoD Directive 7650.3;
therefore, we do not require additional comments.

We appreciate the courtesies extended to the staff. Please direct questions to me at
(703) 604-9187 (DSN 664-9187).

Michael J. Roark
Assistant Inspector General
Contract Management and Payments

Contents

Introduction

Objective

Our objective was to determine whether Space and Naval Warfare Systems Command (SPAWAR) contracting officials provided a fair opportunity to compete, supported price reasonableness determinations, and performed surveillance for task orders issued under multiple-award contracts (MAC) for services, and in accordance with Federal and DoD procedures. This is the fourth in a series of reports addressing the use of MACs for services by DoD activities. See Appendix A for scope and methodology and prior coverage.

Background

SPAWAR Mission and Organization

The Office of the Chief of Naval Operations Instruction 5450.343, updated March 6, 2012, establishes the SPAWAR mission to develop, deliver, and sustain command, control, communications, computers, intelligence, surveillance and reconnaissance (C4ISR) capabilities for warfighters. SPAWAR Headquarters is in San Diego, California. SPAWAR consists of more than 9,500 active duty military and civil service personnel. Through partnerships with three program executive offices, SPAWAR provides the hardware and software to conduct Navy missions. By using its products and services, SPAWAR seeks to transform ships, aircraft, and vehicles from individual platforms into integrated battle forces, enhancing information access and awareness among Navy, Marine, joint forces, Federal agencies, and international allies.

SPAWAR provides support to three Navy Program Executive Offices (PEOs). The program offices within these PEOs work to minimize cost while rapidly delivering products to warfighters. SPAWAR's affiliated PEOs are:

- PEO Command, Control, Communications, Computers and Intelligence;
- PEO Enterprise Information Systems; and
- PEO Space Systems.

SPAWAR is organized into eight competencies:

- Finance,
- Contracts,
- Legal,
- Logistics and Fleet Support,

- Engineering,
- Acquisition and Program Management,
- Science and Technology, and
- Corporate Operations.

Global Installation Contracts

We reviewed the Global Installation MAC, awarded by SPAWAR. The MAC included the following indefinite-delivery indefinite-quantity contracts awarded on February 10, 2011:

- Contract N00039-11-D-0030, awarded to AMSEC LLC for $794,111,857 [AMSEC contract];
- Contract N00039-11-D-0031, awarded to Lockheed Martin Services, Inc. for $831,141,785 [Lockheed Martin contract];
- Contract N00039-11-D-0032, awarded to Serco Inc. for $852,071,894 [Serco contract]; and
- Contract N00039-11-D-0033, awarded to VT Milcom for $843,303,609 [VT Milcom contract].

The MAC was awarded for services to install and certify C4ISR systems onboard surface ships, submarines, and shore stations worldwide. Three contracts had a ceiling price (not to exceed value) of approximately $1.4 billion; however, the AMSEC contract had a ceiling price of $1.3 billion.

The SPAWAR Headquarters contracting office is responsible for contract administration of the four basic MAC contracts and any modifications. The SPAWAR Systems Center (SSC) Pacific and Atlantic are the regional offices responsible for contract administration of task orders and any modifications. Each basic contract included a 3-year base with one 2-year option to extend the period of performance through February 2016. The contracting office exercised the option for all four contracts.

The four contractors competed for task orders under the terms and conditions of the contract. The SPAWAR Headquarters contracting office awarded the first task order in May 2011. As of May 2014, the SPAWAR contracting offices had awarded 622 task orders valued at $356 million.

We reviewed a nonstatistical sample of 20 task orders from the MAC awarded by SPAWAR SSC Pacific valued at $39.7 million. We selected task orders from each contract with a value of $500,000 or more for our review.[1] Our sample included the following task orders by contract:

- AMSEC contract (5 task orders selected, totaling $7,641,158);

- Serco contract (9 task orders selected, totaling $16,943,735); and

- VT Milcom contract (6 task orders selected, totaling $15,125,541).

Review of Internal Controls

DoD Instruction 5010.40, "Managers' Internal Control Program Procedures," May 30, 2013, requires DoD organizations to implement a comprehensive system of internal controls that provides reasonable assurance that programs are operating as intended and to evaluate the effectiveness of the controls. We identified internal control weaknesses at SPAWAR. Specifically, officials did not have procedures in place to ensure contracting officers designated contracting officer's representatives (COR) in a timely manner, verified contractor qualifications, or closed out task orders in a timely manner. We will provide a copy of the report to the senior official responsible for internal controls at SPAWAR.

---

[1] We did not select any task orders from the Lockheed Martin contract because there were no task orders over $500,000 awarded by the SSC Pacific office.

Finding

Most Contracts Were Properly Awarded and Administered but Improvements are Needed

SPAWAR officials generally provided a fair opportunity to compete, supported price reasonableness determinations, and performed surveillance for the nonstatistically selected global installation contracts and 20 task orders in our sample, valued at $39,710,434. In addition, SPAWAR officials generally awarded and managed the task orders in accordance with the Federal Acquisition Regulation (FAR). However, we identified instances where contracting officials could improve their administration of the contract. Specifically, of the 20 task orders reviewed, contracting officials did not:

- properly designate the CORs for two task orders. This occurred because the contracting office did not prepare designation letters before the task order award.

- verify a contractor employee had an Information Assurance Technician certification for one task order. This occurred because contracting personnel relied on the contractor's statement in the proposal and on COR spot checks of contractor's certifications throughout performance of the task order.

- close out a corrective action report (CAR) from 2012 on one of the task orders. This occurred because the onsite Government technician was not properly trained on how to complete a CAR. The SPAWAR official took corrective action during the audit.

- issue the final incentive fee modification to close each task order for five of the eight task orders in our sample where the work had been completed for 10 months or more. This occurred because the contracting office did not always receive the contractor's completion reports, or internal performance reviews and funding reports needed to close out the task order in a timely manner.

As a result, SPAWAR officials increased the risk of using unqualified contractor personnel and overpaying for the services received. In addition, SPAWAR may delay the return of funds that could be put to better use by not performing timely task order closeout actions.

Fair Opportunity, Price Reasonableness Determinations, and Surveillance Were Generally Adequate

SPAWAR officials provided a fair opportunity to compete, supported price reasonableness determinations, and performed surveillance for the global installation contract for most of the 20 task orders in our sample. Specifically, for all 20 task orders, contracting officials provided price reasonableness determinations and, for 19 of the 20 provided fair opportunity to compete and adequate surveillance.[2] See Appendix B for our analysis of the specific task orders. See the following section for more details on the task order that did not have adequate surveillance (AMSEC contract, task order 84).

> SPAWAR officials provided a fair opportunity to compete, supported price reasonableness determinations, and performed surveillance for the global installation contract for most of the 20 task orders in our sample.

For each task order that showed fair opportunity to compete, officials solicited multiple contractors and received multiple proposals. We reviewed:

- performance work statements (PWS) to determine the purpose and scope of the task order;

- requests for proposals to determine the evaluation factors for award; and

- file documentation to determine whether the contracting officer provided all contractors with a fair opportunity to be considered for award.

We verified that for each task order where the contracting officer determined the price to be reasonable, the contracting officer had awarded the task order to the contractor who was technically acceptable with the lowest price. We also examined price evaluations to verify the awardee had the lowest price of the offers received. Finally, we verified whether task orders had adequate surveillance and contained a quality assurance surveillance plan with oversight procedures directly related to the task order.

An example of a task order that met our criteria was contract N00039-11-D-0032, task order 0012. This task order is a performance-based effort that encompasses a wide range of C4ISR[3] installation support services for Shore Naval Tactical

---

[2] One task order (VT Milcom 21) was non-competitive because contracting officials determined it qualified for an exception to the fair opportunity process as a logical follow-on to an order already issued.

[3] Command, Control, Communications, Computers, Intelligence, Surveillance, and Reconnaissance. Supports the development of advanced electronics, communications, surveillance and navigational tools that provide the Navy with a battlefield advantage.

Command Support System hardware and software at various shore locations. The source selection authority based the award of the fixed-price-incentive (firm target) task order on the lowest priced, technically acceptable proposal received. SSC Pacific officials solicited offers from the four MAC contractors; however, they only received one proposal. The contracting office received no-bid responses from the other three contractors. SSC Pacific awarded the task order to Serco on September 1, 2011.

The contracting officer supported price reasonableness for this task order in the task order memorandum. Although there were no other proposals to compare to the price Serco bid, the contracting officer stated in the task order memorandum that the negotiator performed a combination of both price and cost analyses that supported a determination of price reasonableness.

We also verified there was an adequate surveillance plan in place. The overall MAC has a detailed quality assurance surveillance plan (QASP) related to oversight structure and the task order has a QASP with oversight procedures specifically related to the task order.

Contracting Officer's Representatives Were Not Designated

The SPAWAR contracting officer did not properly designate the CORs that were assigned to two task orders, valued at $3.9 million, in compliance with FAR.[4] Specifically, the SPAWAR contracting officer did not provide designation letters in a timely manner to a COR on the AMSEC contract and a COR on the VT Milcom contract.

For the AMSEC contract, task order 84, SPAWAR officials prepared a nomination letter that listed the COR's qualifications and training completed but did not include his proposed duties and responsibilities. The contracting officer awarded task order 84 on December 13, 2013. During our initial site visit in May 2014, we discovered the COR accepted the nomination for this requirement on February 10, 2014, but the contracting officer never provided the COR a designation letter that specified COR responsibilities. According to the SPAWAR contracting official, as of September 5, 2014, the designation letter was in progress. However, on December 4, 2014, the SPAWAR official stated the COR in question was acting

---

[4] FAR Subpart 1.604, "Contracting Officer's Representative."

as the on-site representative and was not the COR. The SPAWAR official stated he updated the performance work statement to include the name of the current COR. SPAWAR Instruction 4200.26C[5] states:

> It is the policy of the SPAWAR Contracting Office at the Contracting Officer's discretion, to designate qualified personnel as their authorized representatives prior to contract award to assist in the technical monitoring and administration of support service contracts.

After the original COR was nominated and named as the COR on two previous revised versions of the performance work statement, a SPAWAR contracting official stated he was not the COR (12 months after officials awarded the task order).

For the VT Milcom contract, task order 79, awarded January 23, 2014, the contracting officer assigned two CORs, but did not provide a designation letter for one of the CORs. During our initial site visit in May 2014, contracting officials stated that the acting COR was an alternate COR. However, one of the CORs stated that there were no alternates and that all CORs performed the same responsibilities for each of the task orders under the contract. Therefore, the contracting officer did not nominate or designate one of the individuals performing COR responsibilities (the acting COR) for the contract.

In addition, the contracting officer for the VT Milcom contract did not provide any of the acting COR's training certificates to verify whether she was properly trained to perform the work. After the acting COR completed COR refresher training in August 2014, the contracting officer designated her as the COR by letter on September 24, 2014 (8 months after awarding the task order).

Problems designating CORs occurred because the contracting office did not prepare COR designation letters before the task order award. While there was no indication that the CORs were not performing their duties effectively, the CORs were not designated by the contracting officer, as required by the FAR. The contracting officer should designate all CORs assigned to perform work on the contract and ensure that all CORs are properly trained before they begin performing COR responsibilities for the task order.

---

[5] SPAWAR Instruction 4200.26C, "SPAWAR Acquisition Procedures," June 3, 2011.

Unverified Contractor Employee Certification

The contracting officer did not verify that a contractor employee had the required Information Assurance Technician Level II (IAT 2) certification for one task order. Specifically, for Serco contract, task order 12, valued at $920,343, the contractor did not provide proof that an employee held the required certification to perform portions of the installation work, as required in the PWS.

The PWS required an Optimized Organizational Maintenance Activity (OOMA) System Analyst with an IAT 2 certification in the Windows operating system and 4 years of experience supporting Naval Aviation Squadrons in the OOMA environment. The proposed Lead System Analyst designated by the contractor for the OOMA System Analyst position had over 23 years of naval aviation experience and advanced Information Technology degrees and certifications. However, the contractor did not provide documentation supporting the information assurance certifications status of the Lead System Analyst required by task 4.1 of the PWS.

The contracting officer stated that the certifications are included in the contractor's quality assurance workbooks (a basic contract requirement). He stated that quality assurance personnel reviewed the workbooks to ensure the certifications were listed and oversight personnel, usually CORs, performed spot checks during execution to ensure the certifications were current. However, for this task order, the contracting officer stated that the COR did not perform spot checks of the contractor's certifications. The contracting officer should revise the quality assurance plan to include methods for the COR to verify that all contractor employees have the required certifications to ensure the Government is receiving what it pays for.

Corrective Action Request Was Not Completed

SPAWAR contracting officials did not close out a 2012 CAR for Serco contract, task order 38. CARs are issued when a Government official identifies a problem that must be addressed by the contractor. According to the Sea Enterprise II Global C4ISR Installation Multiple Award Contract User's Guide, when deficiencies or inadequacies are noted, the COR or Delivery Order COR shall issue a CAR to the contractor advising the contractor in writing within a reasonable time of the contract performance issues. Once the Government official receives the contractor's response to the CAR, they must verify that the contractor's corrective actions adequately addressed the situation and, then close the CAR, or request additional action, if needed.

While conducting fieldwork, we informed SPAWAR officials the CAR issued for task order 38 was not closed out by a Government official. To determine why this CAR was not closed out, we provided the CAR to a SPAWAR official. The official later provided a different copy of the CAR for task order 38 showing it had been closed out in December 2012. The official explained that the closed out CAR he provided documented that SSC Pacific completed the work associated with the CAR in December 2012. The official explained that the initial discrepancy was caused by a training problem. Specifically, he stated that the technical official who recorded the action was not aware that his signature was required to officially close out the CAR. The official stated that SPAWAR now had a completed CAR on file for this problem.

Because the official took corrective action, we are not recommending further action. However, contracting officers need to make sure that all CARs are closed out correctly in the future.

Task Order Closeouts Were Not Completed

Contracting officials did not close out five of the eight task orders in our sample, although the work contracted for in the task orders had been completed for over 10 months. According to the Global Installation MAC statement of work, the task order closeout should take place when the contractor submits all reports and final cost information for the task order. At that time, the COR completes the performance reports in accordance with the quality assurance plan and the contracting officials determine whether the contractors earned the incentive fee.

The contracting officer stated that in some cases the contractors owed the Government money because of cost overruns, or because the Government paid the contractor's incentive fee in advance, but then decided the contractor had not earned the entire fee based on performance. In those cases, the Government must determine the balance of funds due the Government or due the contractor before the task order can be closed out.

For the three task orders that had been closed, the contracting officials issued modifications that provided the final price, including the incentive fee earned. The task orders were:

- AMSEC task order 13: closed out on September 8, 2014, about 14 months after the contractor completed the work, which decreased the total cost of the contract by $26,975.

- Serco task order 12: closed out on May 28, 2013, about 14 months after the contractor completed the work, which decreased the total cost of the contract by $60,814.

- VT Milcom task order 12: closed out on June 10, 2014, about 20 months after the contractor completed the work, which decreased the total cost of the contract by $30,823.

Each decrease in the total cost of each task order represented funds returned to the Government.

Contracting officials stated that task orders were not closed in a timely manner because of either delays in receiving task order completion reports from the contractor or receiving performance reviews and funding reports from the Installation Management Office (IMO). IMO officials stated that the administrative part of the closeout process took longer to complete because it required input from both the contractor and Government. However, the closeout information was needed timely so that the contracting office could calculate the amount of the incentive fee and determine the total final cost. The Global Installation MAC states that the contractors should submit task order completion reports in 90 days or less after the period of performance has ended or after the final modification to fund outstanding Change Order Request Notifications. The contracting officer should promptly contact contractors if they do not submit their task order completion reports in a timely manner. Further, the contracting officer should review and, if necessary, update the task order closeout process to ensure the contracting office closes out the task orders in a timely manner.

Conclusion

Although SPAWAR officials generally provided a fair opportunity to compete, supported price reasonableness, performed surveillance and properly awarded and administered the global installation contract and task orders in our sample, improvements are needed. Officials did not properly designate all CORs, verify all contractor employees had the required certifications, properly track all corrective action requests, or close out task orders in a timely manner. As a result, SPAWAR officials increased performance risk by using potentially unqualified contractor personnel and increased cost risk by potentially paying for expertise not received such as paying for the services

> SPAWAR officials increased performance risk by using potentially unqualified contractor personnel and increased cost risk by potentially paying for expertise not received ...

of more senior technicians than are actually working on the contract. In addition, without corrective action reports, SPAWAR officials may not be able to accurately track contractor corrective actions, and their failure to perform timely task order closeout actions may delay the return of funds that could be put to better use.

Recommendations, Management Comments, and Our Response

Recommendation 1

We recommend that the contracting officer for the Global Installation Contracts:

    a. **Verify that proposed contracting officer's representatives (COR) have completed required training before issuing notices to proceed for each task order.**

Deputy Assistant Secretary of the Navy (Acquisition & Procurement) Comments

The Deputy Assistant Secretary of the Navy (Acquisition & Procurement), responding for the Space and Naval Warfare Systems Command, Global Installation Contracts, Contracting Officer, agreed, stating that Space and Naval Warfare Systems Command's (SPAWAR) documented processes currently require and will continue to require that proposed CORs have completed required training before issuing notices to proceed for each task order. A SPAWAR Contract Department's All Hands email reminder to document COR training prior to award will be sent by March 20, 2015.

Our Response

Comments from the Deputy Assistant Secretary addressed all specifics of the recommendation. SPAWAR issued the reminder email on March 12, 2015. No further comments are required.

    b. **Properly designate all proposed contracting officer's representatives assigned to perform work on the contract by providing contracting officer's representative designation letters that list contracting officer's representative duties and responsibilities.**

Deputy Assistant Secretary of the Navy (Acquisition & Procurement) Comments

The Deputy Assistant Secretary of the Navy (Acquisition & Procurement), responding for the Space and Naval Warfare Systems Command, Global Installation Contracts, Contracting Officer, agreed, stating that SPAWAR currently designates, and will continue to properly designate, all proposed CORs assigned to perform work on the contract by providing COR designation letters that list COR duties and responsibilities, as required by current processes and polices. The requirement for a COR designation letter will be included in the corrective action All Hands email discussed in the response to Recommendation 1.a. above. The email reminder will be sent by March 20, 2015.

Our Response

Comments from the Deputy Assistant Secretary addressed all specifics of the recommendation. SPAWAR issued the remainder email on March 12, 2015. No further comments are required.

    c. **Should revise the quality assurance plan to include methods for the contracting officer's representatives to verify that all contractor employees have the required certifications to ensure the Government is receiving what it pays for.**

Deputy Assistant Secretary of the Navy (Acquisition & Procurement) Comments

The Deputy Assistant Secretary of the Navy (Acquisition & Procurement), responding for the Space and Naval Warfare Systems Command, Global Installation Contracts, Contracting Officer, agreed, stating that the Quality Assurance Surveillance Plan (QASP) will be updated to ensure the task order file is documented to demonstrate that all contractor employees have the required certifications. The revised QASP will require documentation that the COR verified contractor certifications and that the task order file is documented to confirm the certifications were reviewed. SPAWAR plans to finalize the revised QASP by May 29, 2015.

Our Response

Comments from the Deputy Assistant Secretary addressed all specifics of the recommendation, and no further comments are required.

d. Review and, if necessary, update the task order closeout process to ensure the contracting officer closes out all task orders in a timely manner.

Deputy Assistant Secretary of the Navy (Acquisition & Procurement) Comments

The Deputy Assistant Secretary of the Navy (Acquisition & Procurement), responding for the Space and Naval Warfare Systems Command, Global Installation Contracts, Contracting Officer, agreed, stating that the SPAWAR Team remains focused on the task order closeout process. In its January 9, 2015, response to the discussion draft report, SPAWAR updated its automated task order tracking system (Installation Management Office) to track completed task orders and process closeout actions among task order stakeholders. Completed task orders are now visible via the Task Order Closeout Report Queue in the Installation Management Office Tracker. This update provides new visibility of task orders pending closeout and represents an action taken since we conducted our fieldwork.

The SPAWAR Fleet Readiness Directorate is also leading an Integrated Product Team to map out the "As-Is" task order closeout process. The team's focus is to highlight the challenges in the process, identify additional opportunities to improve the process, and recommend changes to SPAWAR management for implementation.

Our Response

Comments from the Deputy Assistant Secretary addressed all specifics of the recommendation, and no further comments are required.

Appendix A

Scope and Methodology

We conducted this performance audit from April 2014 through February 2015 in accordance with generally accepted government auditing standards. Those standards require that we plan and perform the audit to obtain sufficient, appropriate evidence to provide a reasonable basis for our findings and conclusions based on our audit objectives. We believe that the evidence obtained provides a reasonable basis for our findings and conclusions based on our audit objectives.

Universe and Sample Information

We initially queried the Federal Procurement Data System–Next Generation to identify indefinite-delivery contracts that SPAWAR contracting officials awarded from FY 2011 through FY 2013. The queries were not definitive, so we obtained information from the Electronic Data Access System to identify multiple-award, indefinite-delivery contracts for review. We identified one MAC awarded by SPAWAR contracting officials and reviewed the award process, contractor performance, and oversight of the task orders awarded under the MAC. The SPAWAR multiple-award contract included four contracts with a combined not-to-exceed value of $1.4 billion.

We contacted the Quantitative Methods Division to request a sample of task orders to review during our audit fieldwork. We reviewed 15 task orders valued at over $1 million and 5 task orders valued at less than $1 million. We selected a sample of 20 task orders based on high-dollar value. The Quantitative Methods Division recommended that we select the first 15 task orders that were over $1 million and use the population amount of 108 task orders to select the remaining 5 task orders over $500,000.

We reviewed a nonstatistical sample of 20 task orders from the MAC awarded by SPAWAR. We selected task orders from each contract with a value of $500,000 or more for our review.[6] Our sample included the following task orders by contract:

- AMSEC (5 task orders selected, totaling $7,641,158);
- Serco (9 task orders selected, totaling $16,943,735); and
- VT Milcom (6 task orders selected, totaling $15,125,541).

---

[6] We did not select any task orders from the Lockheed Martin contract because there were no task orders over $500,000 awarded by the SSC Pacific office.

Multiple-Award Contracts Reviewed

We reviewed MAC documentation to determine whether SPAWAR contracting officials solicited, awarded, and managed the MACs in accordance with the FAR and other rules and regulations. We reviewed the contract files to determine whether the files represented a complete history of the transactions in accordance with the FAR and SPAWAR policy.

For MAC solicitations we reviewed:

- market research for adequacy and compliance with the FAR and Defense Federal Acqusition Regulation Supplement (DFARS);

- acquisition plans for adequacy of the synopsis, statement of need, acquisition considerations, market research, sources solicited, and set-aside decisions in compliance with the FAR and DFARS;

- statement of work to determine the purpose and scope of the contract; and

- solicitations for adequacy and format, amendments, evaluation factors, and time frames in compliance with the FAR.

For MAC awards, we reviewed:

- proposals to determine whether contractors properly submitted and contracting officials properly handled the proposals in compliance with the FAR;

- technical evaluations for adequacy, completeness, and compliance with the evaluation factors identified in the solicitation and the FAR; and

- price evaluations for adequacy and to determine whether contracting officials established a fair and reasonable price in accordance with the FAR.

For MAC management, we reviewed modifications to determine purpose and cost, and contract files to determine whether contracting officials designated contracting officer's representatives on the overall base contract.

Task Order Documentation Reviewed

We reviewed task order documentation for 20 task orders, valued at $39,710,434, awarded against the MACs to determine whether SPAWAR contracting officers solicited, awarded, and managed the task orders in accordance with the FAR and other rules and regulations. We reviewed the task order files to determine whether the files represented a complete history of the transaction in accordance with the FAR and SPAWAR policy. We also reviewed the files to determine whether SPAWAR contracting officers included final versions of required documentation.

For task order solicitation, we reviewed:

- performance work statements to determine the purpose and scope of the task order,
- requests for proposals to determine the evaluation factors for award, and
- file documentation to determine whether the contracting officer provided all contractors with a fair opportunity to be considered for award in compliance with the FAR and DFARS.

For task order award, we reviewed:

- proposals to determine whether contractors properly submitted, and contracting officials properly handled, the proposals in compliance with the FAR;
- technical evaluations for adequacy, completeness, and compliance with the evaluation factors identified in the request for proposal and the FAR;
- price evaluations for six task orders awarded using the lowest price, technically acceptable method to determine whether the awardee had the lowest price of the offers received;
- source selection decisions for adequacy and completeness; and
- awards to determine the contractors, period of performance, values, type of task order, and terms and conditions.

For task order management, we reviewed modifications to determine purpose, cost, and whether the changes were within the scope of the overall contract and whether contracting officials adequately supported the modification.

We reviewed 20 task orders for contractor performance and customer service satisfaction. We nonstatistically selected the 20 SPAWAR task orders awarded to each of the three SPAWAR MAC contractors. We reviewed the 20 task orders to ensure compliance with the FAR and SPAWAR policy and procedures. Specifically, for the 20 task orders, we reviewed the contents of the contract files to determine if documents were completed and signed. We compared the documentation to the requirements identified in the FAR, DFARS, and other policy. See Appendix C for a complete description of the criteria used.

We obtained position descriptions, and warrants of SPAWAR contracting officials assigned to the SPAWAR MACs and task orders to determine whether they held the appropriate certification and warrant for their position description and in accordance with SPAWAR policy.

The audit team conducted a site visit at SPAWAR Headquarters in San Diego, California. We interviewed contracting officers, contract specialists, and contracting officer's representatives to determine their roles and responsibilities related to the MACs and task orders, customer satisfaction, and contractor performance.

Use of Computer-Processed Data

We did not use computer-processed data to perform this audit.

Use of Technical Assistance

We used the assistance of the Quantitative Methods Division (QMD) specialists to determine which task orders from the contracts awarded from the SPAWAR Global Installation program would best address the audit objectives.

Prior Coverage

During the last 5 years, the Department of Defense Inspector General and the Air Force Audit Agency issued 8 reports discussing the award and administration of Multiple-Award Contracts. Unrestricted DoD IG reports can be accessed at http://www.dodig.mil/pubs/index.cfm. Unrestricted Air Force Audit Agency reports can be accessed from https://www.efoia.af.mil/palMain.aspx by clicking on Freedom of Information Act Reading Room and then selecting audit reports.

DoD IG

DoD IG Report No. DODIG-2013-121, "Award and Administration of Multiple-Award Contracts at Joint Base San Antonio-Lackland Need Improvement," August 23, 2013

DoD IG Report No. DODIG-2013-007, "Award and Administration of Multiple Award Contracts at Naval Facilities Engineering Command Specialty Centers Need Improvement," October 26, 2012

DoD IG Report No. DODIG-2012-134, "Contingency Contracting: A Framework for Reform 2012 Update," September 18, 2012

DoD IG Report No. DODIG-2012-033, "Award and Administration of Multiple Award Contracts for Services at U.S. Army Medical Research Acquisition Activity Need Improvement," December 21, 2011

DoD IG Report No. DODIG-2012-031, "Acquisition Procedures for the Guam Design-Build Multiple Award Construction Contract," December 8, 2011

DoD IG Report No. DODIG-2010-059, "Contingency Contracting: A Framework for Reform," May 14, 2010

Air Force Audit Agency

Air Force Audit Agency Report No. 2013-0009-L30000, "Air Force Center for Engineering and the Environment Support Services Contract Management," April 1, 2013

Air Force Audit Agency Report No. F2011-0008-FC1000, "Multiple-Award Indefinite Delivery Indefinite Quantity Contracts at the Air Logistics Centers," August 13, 2011

Appendix B

Summary of SPAWAR Global Installation Multiple-Award Contract Task Orders

For all 20 task orders, the contracting officials provided price reasonableness determinations. Nineteen of 20 task orders had a fair opportunity to compete and adequate surveillance.

Table 1. AMSEC: N00039-11-D-0030

Task Order	Fair Opportunity	Price Reasonableness Determination	Adequate Surveillance	Task Ongoing (as of 9/30/2014)	Task Order Value
013	Yes	Yes	Yes	No	$ 839,975
063	Yes	Yes	Yes	Yes	2,171,086
065	Yes	Yes	Yes	Yes	771,049
069	Yes	Yes	Yes	No	995,935
084	Yes	Yes	No	Yes	2,863,113
				Total Value:	**$7,641,158**

Table 2. Serco: N00039-11-D-0032

Task Order	Fair Opportunity	Price Reasonableness Determinations	Adequate Surveillance	Task Ongoing	Task Order Value
010	Yes	Yes	Yes	No	$1,007,521
012	Yes	Yes	Yes	No	920,342
036	Yes	Yes	Yes	No	1,138,987
038	Yes	Yes	Yes	No	1,124,821
072	Yes	Yes	Yes	Yes	4,389,888
079	Yes	Yes	Yes	Yes	1,490,245
080	Yes	Yes	Yes	Yes	1,956,352
086	Yes	Yes	Yes	No	1,276,657
109	Yes	Yes	Yes	Yes	3,638,922
				Total Value:	**$16,943,735**

Table 3. VT Milcom: N00039-11-D-0033

Task Order	Fair Opportunity	Price Reasonableness Determinations	Adequate Surveillance	Task Ongoing	Task Order Value
012	Yes	Yes	Yes	No	$ 1,272,691
018	Yes	Yes	Yes	No	5,205,345
021	No	Yes	Yes	No	3,460,704
030	Yes	Yes	Yes	Yes	2,632,821
047	Yes	Yes	Yes	No	1,558,098
079	Yes	Yes	Yes	Yes	995,882
				Total Value:	$15,125,541
Total value of all task orders in our sample (Tables 1, 2 and 3)					*$39,710,434*

Appendix C

Criteria

FAR 1.602-1, "Authority," states, "No contract shall be entered into unless the contracting officer ensures that all requirements of law, executive orders, regulations, and all other applicable procedures, including clearances and approvals, have been met."

FAR 1.602-2, "Responsibilities," states that contracting officers are responsible for ensuring performance of all necessary actions for effective contracting, and shall request and consider the advice of specialists in audit, law, engineering, information security, transportation, and other fields, as appropriate.

FAR2.101, "Definitions," states that the simplified acquisition threshold means $150,000.

FAR 4.801, "General," states:

(a) The head of each office performing contracting, contract administration, or paying functions shall establish files containing the records of all contractual actions.

(b) The documentation in the files (see 4.803) shall be sufficient to constitute a complete history of the transaction for the purpose of —

(1) Providing a complete background as a basis for informed decisions at each step in the acquisition process;

(2) Supporting actions taken;

(3) Providing information for reviews and investigations; and

(4) Furnishing essential facts in the event of litigation or congressional inquiries.

FAR 4.803, "Contents of Contract Files," provides examples of records normally contained in contract files, such as the list of sources solicited, solicitation, proposals, source selection documentation, cost or price analysis, documents supporting modifications, and, in general, "any additional documents on which action was taken or that reflect actions by the contracting office pertinent to the contract."

FAR Subpart 7.1, "Acquisition Plans," 7.000, "Scope of Part," provides policies and procedures for developing acquisition plans. Specifically, 7.102, "Policy," states that agencies shall perform acquisition planning and conduct market research for all acquisitions in order to promote and provide for acquisition of commercial items, full and open competition, and selection of appropriate contract type.

FAR Part 10, "Market Research," 10.000, "Scope of Part," provides the policies and procedures for conducting market research to arrive at the most suitable approach to acquiring supplies and services.

FAR Subpart 15.1, "Source Selection Processes and Techniques," 15.000, "Scope of Part," provides the policies and procedures for competitive and noncompetitive negotiated acquisitions.

FAR Subpart 15.2, "Solicitation and Receipt of Proposals and Information," provides policies and procedures for preparing and issuing requests for proposals and for receiving proposals and requires the use of the uniform contract format.

FAR 15.304, "Evaluation Factors and Significant Subfactors," states:

> The award decision is based on evaluation factors and significant subfactors that are tailored to the acquisition ... the quality of the product or service shall be addressed in every source selection through consideration of one or more non-cost evaluation factors such as past performance ... and past performance shall be evaluated in all source selections for negotiated competitive acquisitions expected to exceed the simplified acquisition threshold.

FAR 15.305, "Proposal Evaluation," states, "Proposal evaluation is an assessment of the proposal and the offeror's ability to perform the prospective contract successfully." It provides further guidance on evaluation cost or price, past performance, and technical abilities.

FAR 15.308, "Source Selection Decision," requires the rationale for the selection decision to be documented.

FAR 15.402, "Pricing Policy," states that contracting officers must purchase supplies and services from responsible sources at fair and reasonable prices.

FAR 15.404-1(e), "Technical Analysis," states:

> At a minimum, the technical analysis should examine the types and quantities of material proposed and the need for the types and quantities of labor hours and the labor mix. Any other data that may be pertinent to an assessment of the offeror's ability to accomplish the technical requirements or to the cost or price analysis of the service or product being proposed should also be included in the analysis.

FAR Subpart 15.5, "Preaward, Award, and Post award Notifications, Protests, and Mistakes," provides guidance for notifying unsuccessful offerors, awarding to successful offerors, conducting pre- and post-award debriefings, and protests.

FAR 16.505(b), "Orders Under Multiple-Award Contracts," states that contracting officers must provide each awardee a fair opportunity to be considered for each order exceeding $3,000 issued under MACs. It also requires each order exceeding the simplified acquisition threshold to be placed on a competitive basis unless supported by a written determination that one of the exceptions to fair opportunity applies. It further identifies exceptions to the fair opportunity process, including "The order must be issued on a sole-source basis in the interest of economy and efficiency because it is a logical follow-on to an order already issued under the contract."

FAR 16.505(b)(7), "Decision Documentation for Orders," states:

> The contracting officer shall document in the contract file the rationale for placement and price of each order, including the basis for award and the rationale for any tradeoffs among cost or price and non-cost considerations in making the award decision. This documentation need not quantify the tradeoffs that led to the decision.

FAR Subpart 42.15, "Contractor Performance Information," 42.1500, "Scope of Part," provides the policies and procedures for recording and maintaining contractor performance information.

FAR 46.407, "Nonconforming Supplies or Services," states that the contracting officer should reject supplies or services that do not conform to the contract requirements.

DFARS 204.802, "Contract Files," states:

> Official contract files shall consist of—
>
> (1) Only original, authenticated or conformed copies of contractual instruments—
>> (i) "Authenticated copies" means copies that are shown to be genuine in one of two ways—
>>> (A) Certification as true copy by signature of an authorized person; or
>>> (B) Official seal.
>> (ii) "Conformed copies" means copies that are complete and accurate, including the date signed and the names and titles of the parties who signed them.
>
> (2) Signed or official record copies of correspondence, memoranda, and other documents.

DFARS 207.103, "Agency-Head Responsibilities," states that agencies must prepare written acquisition plans for acquisitions for services when the total cost is estimated at $50 million or more for all years or $25 million or more for any fiscal year.

DFARS 216.505-70, "Orders under Multiple Award Contracts," states that each order exceeding $150,000 on a MAC must be placed on a competitive basis, unless this requirement is waived on the basis of a justification that is prepared and approved. An order is considered to be placed on a competitive basis only if the contracting officer provides a fair notice of the intent to make the purchase, including a description of the supplies to be delivered or the services to be performed and the basis upon which the contracting officer will make the selection, to all contractors offering the required supplies or services under the multiple award contract. The contracting officer should consider past performance on earlier orders under the contract, including quality, timeliness, and cost control.

Under Secretary of Defense for Acquisition, Technology, and Logistics memorandum, "Implementation Directive for Better Buying Power 2.0 – Achieving Greater Efficiency and Productivity in Defense Spending," April 24, 2013, states acquisition fundamentals include:

(1) effective incentives to industry, especially competitive pressures;

(2) thorough understanding and active management of technical risk;

(3) insistence on demonstrated progress before major commitments;

(4) getting the big early decisions, particularly requirements trade-offs, right; and

(5) using the right contract type for the job.

Management Comments

Deputy Assistant Secretary of the Navy (Acquisition & Procurement) Comments

DEPARTMENT OF THE NAVY
OFFICE OF THE ASSISTANT SECRETARY
(RESEARCH, DEVELOPMENT AND ACQUISITION)
1000 NAVY PENTAGON
WASHINGTON DC 20350-1000

MAR 31 2015

MEMORANDUM FOR DEPARTMENT OF DEFENSE - INSPECTOR GENERAL
ARLINGTON, VIRGINIA

SUBJECT: Department of Defense Inspector General (DODIG) Draft Report
Administration of Space and Naval Warfare Systems Command Global
Installation Multiple-Award Contracts Can Be Improved
(Project No. D2014-D000CN-0163.000)

The Department of the Navy (DON) hereby endorses and forwards the attached
response from Commander, Space and Naval Warfare Systems Command (SPAWAR).
Responses to the Draft Report's recommendations are in Enclosure (1), with supporting
documents provided as Enclosures (2) and (3). Additionally, the Contract's Department
All Hands email referenced in SPAWAR's response to recommendations 1.a and 1.b.
was issued on March 12, 2015, and a copy is provided as Enclosure (4). Accordingly, the
DON believes the corrective action for recommendations 1.a. and 1.b. is complete while
acknowledging that continued oversight and monitoring is required. The DON's
response should be incorporated into the final DODIG report.

If you have any questions pertaining to this memo or its attachments, please refer
them to ██.

Elliott B. Branch

Elliott B. Branch
Deputy Assistant Secretary of the Navy
(Acquisition & Procurement)

Attachments:
As Stated

Copy to:
NAVIG
SPAWAR IG

Deputy Assistant Secretary of the Navy (Acquisition & Procurement) Comments (cont'd)

Space and Naval Warfare Systems Command (SPAWAR)
Response to DoDIG Draft Audit Report
"Administration of Space and Naval Warfare Systems Command
Global Installation Multiple-Award Contracts Can Be Improved"
(Project No. D2014-D000CN-0163.000)

SPAWAR and SPAWAR Systems Center (SSC) Pacific received DoDIG's signed draft report and appreciate the opportunity to comment prior to publication. Following is the list of recommendations and responses.

Recommendation 1
We recommend that the contracting officer for the Global Installation Contracts:

a. Verify that proposed contracting officer's representatives (COR) have completed required training before issuing notices to proceed for each task order.

SPAWAR Response: Concur. SPAWAR's documented processes currently require and will continue to require that proposed CORs have completed required training before issuing notices to proceed for each task order. The contracting officer will ensure the task order file is documented to confirm that a COR has completed the required training prior to issuing a notice to proceed. The required training is listed in the Sample COR Designation Letter found in the SPAWAR Contract Policy and Procedures Manual (SCPPM). The SCPPM is an online tool implementing SPAWAR Instruction 4200.26C, "SPAWAR ACQUISITION PROCEDURES," dated 3 June 2011. The SCPPM is updated regularly to remain current. A copy of SPAWAR Instruction 4200.26C is included as enclosure (2) and a copy of the Sample COR Designation Letter is included as enclosure (3). A SPAWAR Contract's Department All Hands email reminder to document COR training prior to award will be executed by 20 March 2015.

b. Properly designate all proposed contracting officer's representatives assigned to perform work on the contract by providing contracting officer's representative designation letters that list contracting officer's representative duties and responsibilities.

SPAWAR Response: Concur. SPAWAR currently designates and will continue to properly designate all proposed CORs assigned to perform work on the contract by providing COR designation

Enclosure (1)

Deputy Assistant Secretary of the Navy (Acquisition & Procurement) Comments (cont'd)

letters that list COR duties and responsibilities as required by current processes and policies. The contracting officer will ensure the task order file is documented to confirm the issuance of a COR designation letter listing the COR's duties and responsibilities. Oversight of the contract and task orders will continue to be performed by qualified CORs as documented in the COR nomination letter and the COR designation letter. Templates listing the requirements for these letters may be found in the SCPPM. The requirement for a COR designation letter will be included in the corrective action All Hands email discussed in the response to Recommendation 1.a. above. The email will be sent out by 20 March 2015.

c. Should revise the quality assurance plan to include methods for the contracting officer's representatives to verify that all contractor employees have the required certifications to ensure the Government is receiving what it pays for.

SPAWAR Response: Concur. The Quality Assurance Surveillance Plan (QASP) will be updated to ensure the task order file is documented to demonstrate that all contractor employees have the required certifications.

The certifications referenced in the findings are for the cyber security workforce. Section 4.8.6 of the Statement of Work requires the contractors to develop a Quality Assurance (QA) Workbook as a deliverable under the contract. The QA Workbooks contain these certification requirements and document the contractor team's certification levels. The QA Workbooks are checked prior to the contractor beginning work.

In addition to the QA Workbook, SSC Pacific contractors are also required to register their Information Assurance (IA) certificates on the SSC Pacific Cybersecurity Workforce (CSWF) website. Government personnel can check the CSWF site during the technical evaluation or prior to the installation to verify that personnel are certified at required levels. Screen shots from the CSWF website will be provided in separate correspondence.

The revised QASP will require documentation of the COR's check of contractor certifications to ensure the certifications are in place and to ensure the task order file is documented to confirm the certifications were reviewed.

SPAWAR expects to finalize the revised QASP by 29 May 2015.

2

Enclosure (1)

Deputy Assistant Secretary of the Navy (Acquisition & Procurement) Comments (cont'd)

d. Review and, if necessary, update the task order closeout process to ensure the contracting officer closes out all task orders in a timely manner.

SPAWAR Response: Concur. The SPAWAR Team remains focused on the task order closeout process. As communicated to DoDIG in our 9 January 2015 response to the discussion draft report, SPAWAR updated our automated task order tracking system (Installation Management Office (IMO) Tracker) to track completed task orders and workflow the closeout actions among the task order stakeholders. Screen shots from the IMO Tracker system will be provided in separate correspondence. Completed task orders are now visible via the added button entitled, "Task Order Closeout Report Queue (TOCR Q)" in the Installation Management Office Tracker (IMOTracker). This update provides new visibility of task orders pending closeout and represents an action taken since DoDIG conducted their fieldwork.

The SPAWAR Fleet Readiness Directorate (FRD) is also leading an Integrated Product Team (IPT) to map out the "As-Is" task order closeout process. This team meets bi-weekly to sustain the review of the task order closeout process. The team's focus is to highlight the challenges in the process, identify additional opportunities to improve the process, and recommend changes to SPAWAR management for implementation.

SPAWAR believes the corrective action is complete, but will continue to monitor the closeout status of open orders.

3   Enclosure (1)

Acronyms and Abbreviations

C4ISR   Command, Control, Communications, Computers, Intelligence, Surveillance, and Reconnaissance

CAR   Corrective Action Request

COR   Contracting Officer's Representative

DFARS   Defense Federal Acquisition Regulation Supplement

FAR   Federal Acquisition Regulation

IAT 2   Information Assurance Technician Level II

IMO   Installation Management Office

MAC   Multiple-Award Contract

OOMA   Optimized Organizational Maintenance Administration

PEO   Program Executive Office

PWS   Performance Work Statement

QASP   Quality Assurance Surveillance Plan

SPAWAR   Space and Naval Warfare Systems Command

www.ingramcontent.com/pod-product-compliance
Lightning Source LLC
Chambersburg PA
CBHW081138280526
45787CB00007B/3132